GERALDINE COTTER'S

Traditional Irish Tin Whistle Tutor

To access audio, visit:
www.halleonard.com/mylibrary

1997-8372-4141-6881

ISBN 978-1-84609-807-9

O S S I A N

EXCLUSIVELY DISTRIBUTED BY

Visit Hal Leonard Online at
www.halleonard.com

World headquarters, contact:
Hal Leonard
7777 West Bluemound Road
Milwaukee, WI 53213
Email: info@halleonard.com

In Europe, contact:
Hal Leonard Europe Limited
Dettingen Way
Bury St Edmunds, Suffolk, IP33 3YB
Email: info@halleonardeurope.com

In Australia, contact:
Hal Leonard Australia Pty. Ltd.
4 Lentara Court
Cheltenham, Victoria, 3192 Australia
Email: info@halleonard.com.au

'For John, le grá mór'

The publishers wish to extend their thanks to the many institutions
and individuals whose kind and generous assistance is greatly appreciated.
Special thanks are due to:
Michael Ó Suilleabhain, Tomas Ó Canainn,
Comhaltas Ceoltóiri Éireann for the photographs of Hugh Rushe &
Brid O'Donoghue.
The Traditional Irish Music Archive for pictures of Micho Russell,
Liam Jordan for his photographs of Mary Bergin & Sean Ryan.
Gill & MacMillan for the use of the (adapted) designs from
'Songs of Uladh' by John Campbell.
Line drawing of Geraldine Cotter by Norah O'Driscoll.
Diagrams by John Boyd.
Music origination by Andrew Shiels.
Design and layout by John Loesberg
Cover artwork by Joe Gervin.

Index

Geraldine Cotter is one of the new breed of young Irish traditional musicians — authentic, innovative and highly talented. She has acquired by birth and opportunity the undiluted tradition of her native Clare.

Geraldine was awarded the Comhaltas Ceoltóiri Éireann scholarship to University College Cork, and has participated in the CCE Concert Tour of North America. Her success as a teacher of Irish traditional music is well attested to by the lucky students who have had the benefit of her tuition.

Labhrás Ó Murchú
Ard - Stiurthoir, Comhaltas Ceoltóiri Éireann

Introduction

The Tin Whistle is probably the most widely used instrument for playing Irish Traditional Music. It is the cheapest and easiest to play. It is possible to play all forms of Traditional Music on it including all the techniques of ornamentation. It is therefore ideal for the beginner to start with.

There are two types of Tin Whistle in use today. The first is the 'Clarke's C' Whistle, which is made of tin with an underlip of wood set into the head. The shape is conical or tapered. It has a very pleasing tone but is only available in the key of C, making it suitable for solo playing only .

The second type of Whistle is the cylindrical 'D' Whistle, consisting of a metal column with a plastic mouthpiece. This is the most popular type in use. The mouthpiece is moveable so you can tune to other instruments, i.e. concertina, pipes, etc.

How to use this book

This book may be used in conjunction with audio tracks, available online (see p. 1). First of all play the audio through a couple of times so you become familiar with the music. Start at the beginning of the book, do not try to master something too difficult.

The material that is covered in this tutor varies from simple tunes (polkas etc.) up to more complex pieces. There is a special discussion of the Slow Airs. All the basic techniques necessary to master the Tin Whistle are here, including ornamentation, variation, etc. You are shown how to introduce them into a tune.

Do not rely on the printed music alone, Irish Music is an aural tradition and if played from music alone becomes sterile, but notation used in conjunction with a recording can be an aid in learning to play this music.

There is a Discography at the end of the book, also a list of sources of further tunes. Some addresses are also given for reference.

Important note :   **a 'D - tuning' Tin Whistle is the required instrument to be used with this tutor.**

chapter 1

Music

Music for any melodic instrument used in traditional Irish music is written on a group of five lines and four spaces. This is called **a stave**. At the beginning of each line there is a sign called a **treble clef**. The position of the notes on the stave records the pitch of the notes, while the shape of the notes show the rhythm and time value of each.

Highness and Lowness

When we talk about high notes and low notes in music we use the word **pitch**. The stave works like steps on a ladder, each line and each space on the stave is a step. Each step is a different pitch. When we see a note on the stave we will know exactly which note to play on the whistle because each has its name taken from the first seven letters of the alphabet.

The notes **on the spaces** are called F A C E

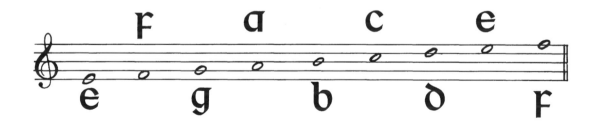

The notes **on the lines** are called E G B D F, remembered easily by :

Every Good Boy Deserves Football.

Sounds often go higher or lower than the pitches on the stave, when this happens **leger lines** are used to write these notes on :

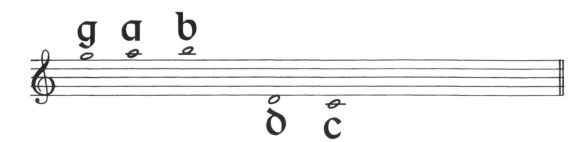

When notes go up or down a step at a time they play a **scale**.
In fact the word scale comes from the Italian word *scala*
which means ladder.

Scale of D - beginning on D and finishing on D.

Relating all this to the tin whistle :

Holding the tin whistle

Hold the mouthpiece between your lips (Don't chew it !), blow
gently but evenly to get a clear sound.

Covering the holes

The fingers 2, 3, and 4 of your **left hand** are used to cover the top
three holes of the whistle, i.e. the holes nearer the mouthpiece.
The fingers 2, 3, and 4 of your **right hand** are used to cover the
remaining three holes.

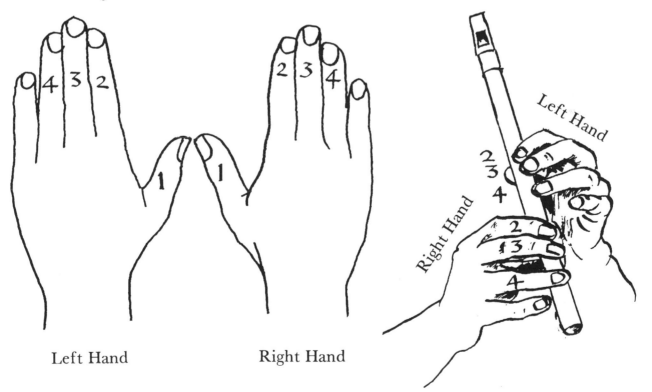

Left Hand   Right Hand

The little finger of the right hand can be placed on the whistle to help
balance it. The two thumbs are placed behind the whistle opposite
finger no. 2 in each hand.

The pitch sounded on a D tin whistle
when all holes are covered is D; written :

A **high** note D' can also be sounded in the
same manner but by blowing a little harder.
As you can see from the next chart this note
can also be fingered differently.

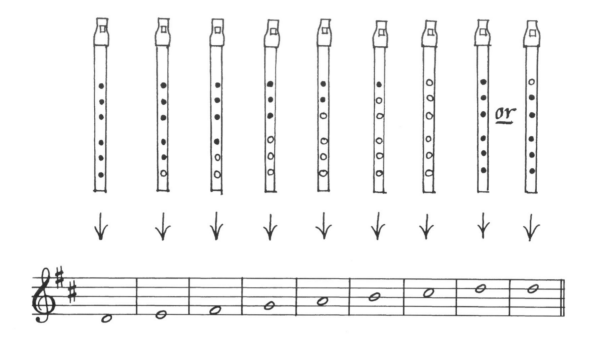

Now practise playing the scale of D. Practise going up first, and when
you feel confident with this try coming down. When going up the scale
remember you are taking off one finger at a time from the bottom.
Coming down you are mostly putting down fingers from the top hole.

To achieve confidence with blowing and co-ordination
of fingers try these exercises : —

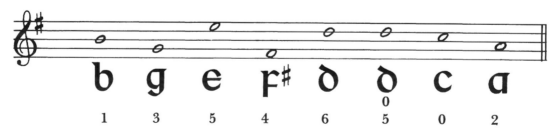

B1 means that the note B is played with one finger down.
G3 means that the note G is played with three fingers down, etc.
The consecutive series of notes is called the **scale of D.**

This constitutes the first **octave** (& notes) of the D tin whistle. The second octave is obtained by using the same fingering as the first octave but blowing harder.

d e f♯ g a b c♯

chapter 2

Tongueing

Before we go any further, learn the tongueing technique.
This enables you to produce a clean start and end to each note.
Put your tongue up against the roof of your mouth (back of
your upper teeth) then when you blow out drop your tongue gently.
Now try this tune :

ailiú eanái

6 6 6 6 1 2 4 2 1 1 1 1 1 2 4 2 2 4 6 5 4 5 6 6
D D D D B A F A B B B B B A F A A F D E F E D D

Try to learn the notes of this tune without relying too much on
the numbers. This tune is based on the notes of the first octave.
Next try this tune which uses notes from the second octave : --

ím bím babaró

Here is another simple tune which you can try.

The above tune is a **polka** . This type of tune is played in
counties such as Kerry, Cork, Waterford and Wexford, to which
the 'set' is danced.

chapter 3
Time & Rhythm

So far we have dealt solely with the pitch of notes, another aspect of music which we have to deal with is 'duration' or as it commonly is called : — time.

Note values

o	called either **whole note** or **semibreve**	4 Beats : count 1 - 2 - 3 - 4
𝅗𝅥	called either **half note** or **minim**	2 Beats : count 1 - 2
♩	called either **quarter note** or **crotchet**	1 Beat : count 1
♪	called either **eighth note** or **quaver**	½ Beat
♬	called either **sixteenth note** or **semiquaver**	¼ Beat

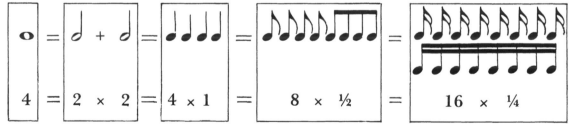

Time Signatures

Music is divided into **bars** . Normally in Irish Traditional Music there are 8 bars in each section of a tune, at the end of each section there is a **double bar** , sometimes there is a sign like this, :‖ which means that the section is repeated. See the polka learned in chapter 1. Where a bar line is placed depends on the **time signature** of the piece. A time signature is a set of numbers written at the beginning of a piece of music : —

3   The top number tells you the **number of beats** in a bar.

4   The bottom number tells you the **type of beats** in a bar.

e.g. **3/4** , there are three ¼ note (crotchet) beats in a bar.

e.g.

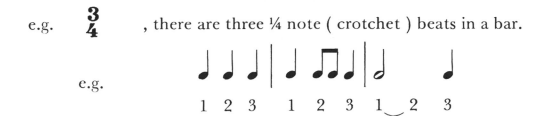

1 2 3   1 2 3   1 ⌣ 2 3

A dot after a note makes it half as long again.

e.g. 𝅗𝅥. = 𝅗𝅥 + ♩ =   2 + 1 = 3 beats.

Try in **4/4** time :

count : 4 and   1, 2 and 3, 4 and 1, 2, 3, 4 and 1, 2 and 3, 4 and 1,2,3

Examples of Time Signatures

2/4   2 beats in a bar — found in **Marches, Polkas**

3/4   3 beats in a bar — found in **Waltzes, Airs & Songs**

4/4   4 beats in a bar — found in **Marches, Reels, Hornpipes & Set Dances**

4/4   Time is often indicated by **C**

6/8   6 quavers in a bar — found in **Jigs & Set Tunes**

9/8   9 quavers in a bar — found in **Slip Jigs**

12/8   12 quavers in a bar — found in **Slides & Single Jigs**

In 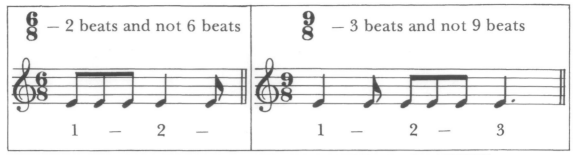 the quavers are grouped in 3's so that in :

$\frac{6}{8}$ — 2 beats and not 6 beats

$\frac{9}{8}$ — 3 beats and not 9 beats

$\frac{12}{8}$ — 4 beats and not 12 beats

The rhythm of a jig is easily learnt by the rhythm of the words :
Humpty Dumpty sat on the wall

example : —

the Milltown jig

* See page 29

Try this **Slip Jig** : —

nead na lachan sa mhúta

Try this **March** : —

Clare's Dragoons

chapter 4

A note on breathing

After playing a few tunes you have probably found it difficult to control your breathing. The solution is to assign certain 'breathing points' to the tune. It will become more natural after a while, like the **unconscious breathing you do when speaking.** After taking a breath, remember not to lose the rhythm of the tune. e.g. The 2nd half of the polka : —

The symbol ⅞ is a **rest** and means no note is played. In the above (i), instead of playing the high A you can take a breath, as in e.g. (ii). This will help the rhythm and also add variation to the piece. Instead of slipping a pause between the notes eliminate one of the notes entirely and use that space for a breath.

It is not possible to make any hard and fast rules concerning breathing and **phrasing** but in general breaths are taken at the end of the 2nd, 4th, 6th or 8th bars of a tune. Experience will tell you where to do this.

Another point to remember is that even though it is possible to play a large part of a tune without taking a breath, it is not the most attractive thing to hear — it leads to a certain monotony in the music.

Tunes in the key of D have two sharps
at the beginning of a piece : C♯ and F♯

d e f♯ g a b c♯ d e f♯ g a b

We will now deal with the key of G.
The key of G has one sharp i.e. — F♯

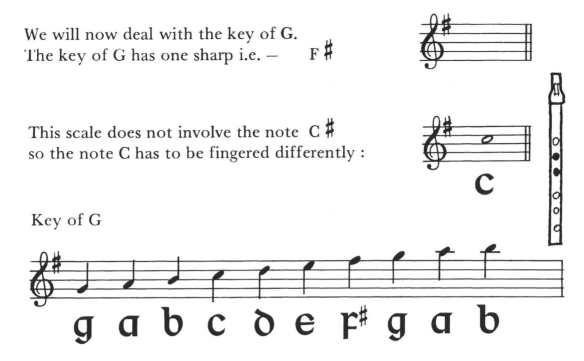

This scale does not involve the note C♯
so the note C has to be fingered differently :

Key of G

g a b c d e f♯ g a b

Try this tune in the key of G : —

Donal na Gréine

B C B

Going from B to C and vice - versa is quite difficult at first but if you
isolate this section and practise it, it will be easier. In the above tune,
practise bar 3 and you should have no trouble with the rest.

Here is another tune in G : —

green grow the rushes o

Here are two **Polkas** to try : —

Balleydesmond No.1

18

Balleydesmond No. 2

chapter 5
Articulation

Articulation is the way in which a note is 'attacked'.
This is an important aspect of whistle playing ; the tongue, mouth
and the fingers are all used in this technique. Different styles use
different methods of articulation, e.g. compare the style of Miko Russell
to that of Mary Bergin or Willie Clancy.

Tongueing

Tongueing is a form of articulation very common in tin whistle playing.
We have touched briefly on it before, we will recapitulate on it.
Play a note on the tin whistle and hold it, move your tongue to the
roof of your mouth while blowing. This of course stops the flow of
air which in turn stops the note from sounding. Introduced at the
appropriate time in a piece it can be very effective. Tongueing has the
effect of giving a light accent to a note.

Vibrato

Vibrato is another form of articulation. This is a slight 'wavering' of
the pitch of a note, it is very commonly used in Slow Airs to give a
nice effect. It can be done by controlling the flow of air from the
throat or by shaking the finger that is two or more holes below the
note played. Used too often however, it loses its effect. Anyone
familiar with European Art Music will have come across the term 'vibrato'.

Staccato & Legato

The use of **staccato** or **legato** in tin whistle playing varies ; generally
a player is either using one or the other. A legato player could be one
using less tongueing and a more smooth, unbroken type of style.
A staccato player would have more use of tongueing, strongly
accented. Again, listening to various players will make you familiar
with both styles. Listen to some of the recordings **listed at the end**
of the book.

Slurring

Slurring is a very common form of articulation. More than any of the forms this should not be over - used. In the appropriate place its use can be very effective. This is achieved by sliding into the note from the note below.

Slurring is most effective in Slow Airs and helps to create an atmosphere.

In the next tune I have marked in where one could use the particular forms of articulation so far discussed. It is important to note that it is only one example and many different approaches can be made.
Notes using a slur are all linked together (no tongueing).
Detached notes have no slur over them (tongueing).

A dot over or under a note means ' staccato ' e.g.

Notes which are slurred have an arrow under or over them

Ornamentation has not yet been included in the tune

apples in winter

Variations on bars 6 - 7

Variation

Much more variation can be used. Each time you repeat the same piece it can be played differently, this will be gone into in greater detail later in the book. Naturally enough this will be different from player to player. This is only an example of how it can be played. With the inclusion of ornamentation it would be even different. These are the basic ways of articulating a note : —
Tongueing, Vibrato, Staccato & Legato, Slurring

chapter 6
Ornamentation

Ornaments are used to decorate or embellish a melody.
If used in the correct way they can enhance a tune and make it more interesting to listen to. When you have mastered the technique of ornamentation there is a danger of over - using it. If you listen to recordings of accomplished players (see Discography) and become familiar with the idiom, the danger of over - ornamentation is reduced. The tin whistle is suited to ornamentations such as the **casadh, cuts & rolls.** Much practise is needed to control these techniques.

the Cut

This is an easy and very subtle form of ornamentation, cuts can be used on the notes D, E, F♯ , G , A and B

       Cut by A   Cut by C♯

As you can see, the notes D, E, F and G are cut by A, the others are cut by C♯ . The method is the same on the second octave of the whistle.

To play a cut on , say D, you don't have to actually remove all four fingers to play A. It suffices just to 'twitch' the finger on the 3rd hole.

Slightly move or 'twitch' the finger on this hole

The ornament is literally 'cut' into the main note — The emphasis being on the main (D) note.

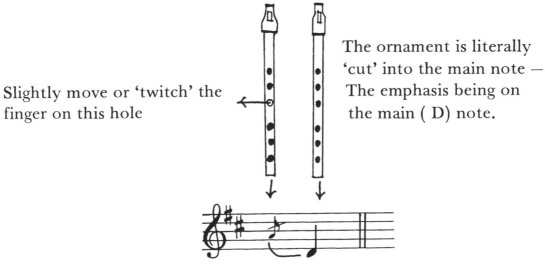

A cut on the D note

the Casadh

The **casadh** is similar to the cut exept that the principal note is also part of the ornament, e.g.

Try the following : —

Dingle regatta

the Roll

The **roll** is one of the more attractive types of ornamentation used in Irish music. Used in the right place it can enhance the tune but care must be taken not to over - use it. The following are examples of rolls, as in the 'cut' it is not necessary to raise all the fingers to play the notes of the ornament.

E roll   F♯ roll   G roll   A roll   B roll

Rolls are possible only on five notes of the scale : E, F♯ , G, A , B. Another thing to keep in mind when playing rolls is that only the main note is 'tongued'. Make sure all parts of the roll are heard. The examples given above can be used mainly in jigs to replace a dotted crotchet or ♩.

Try the rolls in ' The Dingle Regatta '

dotted   =   E roll   A roll
crotchet

Another very common type of roll is on a crotchet (♩) and is used a good deal in Reels. It quite often comes in the middle of a bar after a group of quavers, this is how they are played : —

played   played   played   played   played

Seaġan· mac Cazmaoil·vel.

Try the following reel, putting in rolls where marked

the Longford collector

Triplets

A **triplet** is a group of three notes played in the time of two, e.g. —

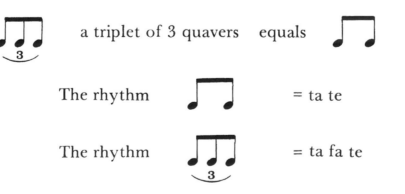

a triplet of 3 quavers   equals

The rhythm   = ta te

The rhythm   = ta fa te

Triplets are often used to link notes a third apart e.g. —

   could be varied

chapter 7

putting it all together

In this chapter I will deal with the question of variation. I will first present the tune in its basic form and then give some examples of variation techniques. Variation can be ornamental, melodic and rhythmic. Finally, I will give a possible arrangement of the tune.

It must be kept in mind that notated music has its limitations. The ideal way of learning this music is to listen to different recordings of reputable players. It is necessary to immerse yourself completely in the music, listening constantly to different styles, in order to develop your own style. The arrangements given here are only simple versions of the tune (s) and should not be copied note for note.

The idea in this chapter is to give an explanation of what variation consists of. A player should strive towards his/her own individual version of a tune. Variation should come naturally in an improvisory manner, from an understanding of the techniques used in the Tradition.

It is better that only minor variations done at ease be attempted, rather than complicated, calculated attempts that sound laboured. Irish Traditional Music is a highly developed living art form, if possible try to listen to a musician 'live', you will find a whistle player will play a **tune** different every time, constantly introducing new ideas, ornamentation, variation etc.

common faults
in whistle playing

a) Playing the tune too fast.

b) Learning one version of the tune and ignoring all others.

c) Developing one aspect of the performance of the tune and forgetting all others.

The first tune which I'll introduce is the Milltown Jig, a Double Jig in 2 parts. I would suggest that the tune is learned in its basic form before tackling any ornamentation or variation. Once you gain experience and confidence these techniques will come naturally. However, when learning an instrument great patience is required.

(i) the milltown jig

Looking at the first half of the tune you will notice that bars 1, 3 & 5 are identical. If they were to be played like this each time the piece would be boring and monotonous. Some alternatives could be melodic or ornamental e.g. instead of : —

one could play any of the following : —

As you can see looking at the basic tune there is a variation already built into the second half of the jig. Remember when playing the tune you play the first 4 bars of the second half,

then the 4 bars under ⌐1.

then repeat the first 4 bars of the second half, this time playing the 4 bars under ⌐2.

I will now give an example of a possible rendering of the tune incorporating some of the variation and ornamentation techniques discussed. I will not write out rolls in full but instead use the symbol ♩ The symbol for a slide up to a note is an arrow e.g. ♩ or ♩

(ii) the milltown jig

the Reel

The next tune we will look at is called 'Ladies Pantalettes'. This is a **single reel**, unlike the jig which was double. **Each** part is played once. As with the jig the best way to approach this reel is to first learn the basic tune. Do not attempt the ornamentation until you feel fairly confident with the basic tune.

(i) ladies pantalettes

Looking at the tune you will notice that in the first half bars
1, 3, 5, and 7 are similar. In the second half bars 9, 11, 13 and 15 are
alike. Here are some ways of varying the first half : —

can be played   or

Some ways of varying the second half : —

can be played   or

On the next page is a possible version of the tune with some rolls, casadh,
cuts, slides etc. included. As stated earlier — do not think of this as the
only way to play the tune. It is only one way and there are many more
ways. However, it will serve as a good guideline.

The Slide into a note is quite often used in conjunction
with a roll, e.g. in the opening bar : —

slide
G roll

Seaġan· mac Caṫmaoil· del.

(ii) ladies pantalettes

the Hornpipe

Here are two **hornpipes** — 'Tomorrow Morning' and the 'Feis Hornpipe'. Again I have given one possible way of playing them but do try to get away from the written version.

tomorrow morning

(i)   basic tune

(ii)   with ornaments

the Feis hornpipe

basic tune   (i)

with ornaments   (ii)

chapter 8

Slow Air playing

In my view a tutor on Irish Music would not be complete without a mention of **slow airs**. Much of our culture is associated with the Songs and Airs of Ireland. Quite often musicians concentrate on one aspect and ignore the other. Musicians who play dance music sometimes ignore the whole idea of Airs. The playing of Airs is something which requires special study. Each Air must be treated individually. The best way to approach it is to study the background to the Air. Most Airs have their origin in songs, so the easiest way to study one is to listen to a good performance of the song. To keep the notated version is not satisfactory since Airs cannot be transcribed or accurately notated, even if they were, they would look extremely complicated on paper. Even though the metre is not lost there is sometimes a lengthening or shortening of notes which allows freedom from the barline. On listening to a good **Sean -nos** singer performing a song, one will notice that the notes which are lengthened are often associated with important words of the song. For this reason, it is important to be conscious of words. When the words aren't known study the atmosphere of the melody, its phrasing, climaxes etc. Sensitivity and Feeling are prime ingredients to good Air playing, all the technique in the world is not sufficient on its own.

The technical things to keep in mind are :

        a)   To be conscious of breathing
        b)   Use of pauses
        c)   Over - use of ornamentation

Ornamentation should be used to enhance a tune.

In Air playing it should relate as far as possible to that of the song.

Likewise breathcontrol should correspond to that used during the singing of the Air. A fairly good guide as to where to take a breath — is at the end of each phrase (usually eight bars). Sometimes one can be taken after four bars.

Many of the songs of Ireland are associated with love and misfortune. An example of one such song is ' Na Connerys'. The Connerys were sent to New South Wales for their involvement in sheep stealing.

na Connerys

A Choi-mín mhal-laithe — guím -se deac- air ort a - gus

gráin Mhic Dé ar an ghas- ra úd atá

ceangailte go dlúth le d' thaobh ; 's iad a dhearbhaigh na

leabharta go humhal sa mbréag, do chuir na Conn-er-ys thar na

far-raig-ibh go dtí na New South Wales.

na Connerys

' = Breathing points, Ends of phrases.

The next tune ' Molly St George ' was composed by Thomas Connellan
a harper - composer of the late 1600's born in Cloonmahon, Co. Sligo.
Molly St George is said to have been of the St George family of Co. Leitrim.

Molly St.George

Another example is 'Casadh an tSugain'. (Twisting the hayrope). According to the story, a young man comes courting the woman of his heart. She asks him to show how well he can twist a hay-rope. He keeps adding hay and twisting away and backing up as he twists until he is outside the door and she slams it in his face. He hates her for tricking him. He protests he is a better man than most . He shudders to think he will have to marry a plain girl for her money. And he reflects bitterly on the woman he has lost. Such is the confusion that reigns in the heart of a man who has been jilted. The well known 'Rocks of Bawn' tune is constructed on the latter half of this melody. The song's story formed the subject of the first Gaelic play performed in Dublin ' Casadh an tSugain' by Douglas Hyde.

Casadh an tSúgáin

Conclusion

Having worked through this tutor you will probably want to extend your repertoire of tunes. The author has prepared a collection of 100 tunes which you will find in the appendix to the tutor. These tunes have been collected in Clare, Galway, Cork & Kerry from traditional musicians. Most of the tunes have never before appeared in print.

The tunes in this tutor are widely played by traditional whistle players. You will find each musician has his/her own style, depending on the region. Each musician will use varying ornamentation etc. Do not take one particular version of a tune as the 'correct' one, especially if it's from a book. Learn the basic tune, then with an understanding of the techniques in this tutor, build up the tune. Try to listen to as much whistle playing as you can from all sources ; — records, live performances, concerts, etc. Try to develop your ear by learning tunes off records. Learning traditional Irish Music is like serving an apprenticeship, it takes time but the end results are worth it.

Bibliography

Further sources of tunes : —

1. The Roche Collection of Traditional Irish Music, 566 Irish Airs, Marches and Dance tunes suitable for most instruments. *Ossian*
2. Ceol Rince na hEireann, Vols 1 & 2 by Brendan Breathnach, *Government Printing office. Arcade G.P.O. Dublin.*
3. The Dance Music of Willie Clancy, by Pat Mitchell. *Ossian*
4. O' Neill's Music of Ireland 1001 Melodies, *Walton's, Dublin.*
5. O' Neill's Music of Ireland 1850 Melodies, *Dan Collins, New York.*
6. An Piobaire, Nos 1 - 34, 1971-8 in 1 vol . *Ceol an Phiobaire, from Na Piobairi Uilleann, 15 Henrietta St. Dublin 1.*

Discography

The following recordings are completely devoted to the tin whistle:

1. Mary Bergin - FEADÓGA STÁIN (Gael Linn) *CEFCD 071*
2. DONNCHA Ó BRIAN (Gael Linn) CEFC 083
3. TOM McHALE (Outlet) *OLP 1001*
4. Paddy Moloney, Sean Potts - TIN WHISTLES (Claddagh) *CC15CD*
5. TOTALLY TRADITIONAL TIN WHISTLES - Fintan Vallely, Miko Russell, Willie Clancy, John Doonan, Josie McDermott, Michael Tubridy and Cathal McConnell. (Ossian) *OSSCD53*

The Following recordings featurevarious artists/instruments:

6. Willie Clancy - THE MINSTREL FROM CLARE (Ossian) *OSSCD23*
7. Michael Tubridy - THE EAGLE'S WHISTLE (Claddagh) *CC27CD*
8. Micho Russell - TRADITIONAL MUSIC OF CO.CLARE (Free Reed) *FRR004A*
9. DARBY'S FAREWELL - Josie McDermott (Ossian) *OSSCD20*
10. MUSIC FROM THE COLEMAN COUNTRY - Jim Donaghue, John Joe Mooney (Leader) *LEA 204411*
11. FOLKSONGS OF IRELAND - Seamus Ennis (Ember) *2504*
12. THE RUSSELL FAMILY OF DOOLIN, Co.Clare (Ossian) *OSSCD8*
13. SEODA CEOIL 1 - Willie Clancy (Gael Linn) *CEF018*

a collection of 100 tunes
consisting of jigs, reels, hornpipes,
set dances, slow airs &
miscellaneous pieces,
all suitable for the tin whistle.
ornamentation is left to the
discretion of the player

1. THE RETURNED YANK

2. BANISH MISFORTUNE

3. TOM FRIELS

4. HARRY'S LOCH

5. DONNYBROOK FAIR

6. GILLIAN'S APPLES

7.   THE HAIRPIN BEND

8.   DAN THE COBBLER

9.   THE BURNT OLD MAN

10.   DOWN THE BACK LANE

11.   THE MUG OF BROWN ALE

12.   MOLLOY'S FAVOURITE

13. THE MONAGHAN JIG

14. TOBIN'S

15. DO YOU WANT ANYMORE ?

16. THE IDLE ROAD

17. SHORES OF LOUGH GOWNA

18. RYAN'S FAVOURITE

19. LANGSTROM'S PONY

20. THE BOYS OF THE TOWN

21. AUSTIN BARRETT'S

22.   THE OLD GREY GOOSE

56

23. PADDY CANNEY'S NO. 1

24. PADDY CANNEY'S NO. 2

SLIP JIGS

25. HUNTING THE HARE

26. OPEN THE DOOR

27. I HAVE A WIFE OF MY OWN

28. THE HUMOURS OF KILKENNY

29. DEVER THE DANCER

60

30. DROPS OF SPRING WATER

31. AN PHIS FLIUCH

61

32. WILL YOU COME DOWN TO LIMERICK

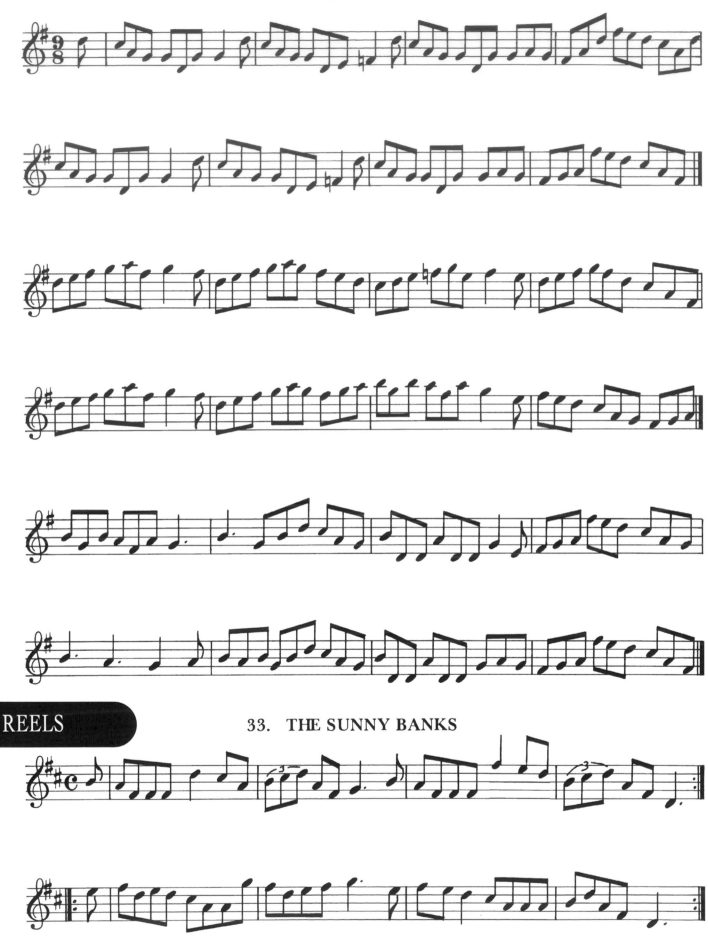

REELS

33. THE SUNNY BANKS

34. THE DRUNKEN LANDLADY

35. LONDON LASSES

36. TOMMY MC MAHON'S

37. DOWN THE BROOM

38.   MISS MONAGHAN

39.   LUCKY IN LOVE

40. IN THE TAP ROOM

41. THE PEELER'S JACKET

42. THE FLOWERS OF LIMERICK

43. THE BURREN NO. 1

44. THE GOLDEN KEYBOARD

45. THE GALWAY RAMBLER

46. THE KERRY REEL

47. KING OF THE CLANS

69

48. THE SHEPHERD'S DAUGHTER

49. SHUFFLE THE CARDS

50. THE OLD BUSH

51. AH, SURELY

71

52. THE GREEN MEADOW

53. LUCY CAMPBELL

54. THE BANK OF IRELAND

55. THE JOLLY BANGER

56. THE CONTROVERSIAL REEL

57. KILFENORA NO. 1

58. KILFENORA NO. 2

59. THE BELL HARBOUR

60. BLACKBERRY BLOSSOM

61.   THE ROVER THROUGH THE BOG

62.   THE KINGSTOWN HORNPIPE

63. SONNY MURRAY'S

64. THE CLAREMAN'S HORNPIPE

65.   THE WREN'S HORNPIPE

66.   DUNPHY'S HORNPIPE

67.   GAN AINM

68.   GAN AINM

69. THE PLAINS OF BOYLE

70. CHIEF O' NEILL'S

71.   THE FAIRIES' HORNPIPE

72.   THE STACK OF WHEAT

73. OFF TO CALIFORNIA

74. WILLY WALSHE'S HORNPIPE

75.   THE ORANGE ROGUE

76. THE BLACKBIRD

77. BONAPARTE'S RETREAT

78.   THE JOB OF JOURNEYWORK

79. THE GARDEN OF DAISIES

80. THE ACE & DEUCE OF PIPERING

F ♮ (natural) is played by half - covering the hole.

81. THE DRUNKEN GAUGER

82. THE RAMBLING RAKE

83. AN SÚISCIN BÁN

84. THE LODGE ROAD

85. ANACH CUAIN

86. BRUACH NA CARRAIGE BAINE

87. CATH CHÉIM AN FHIA

88.   URCHNOC CHÉIN MHIC CÁINTE

89. AN GOIRTÍN EORNA

90. AN MHAIGHDEAN MHARA

91.   COINLEACH GLAS AN FHOMHAIR

92.   AN BUACHALL CAOL DUBH

93. FATH MO BHUARTHA

94. CAILÍN NA GRUAÍGE DOINNE

95. AMHRÁN A LEABHAIR

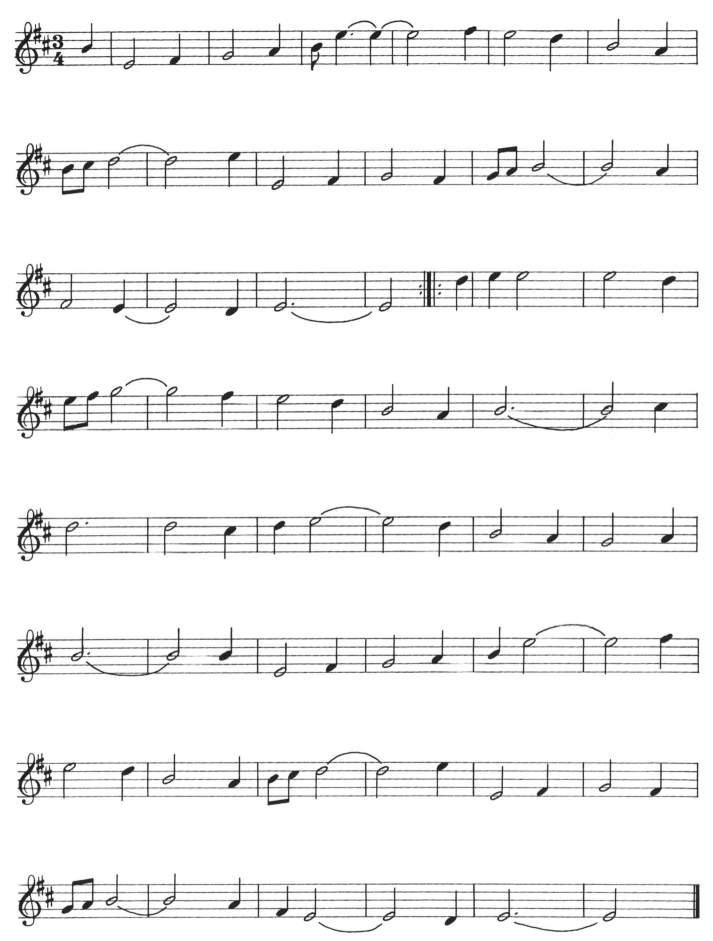

96. THE CUMANN NA mBAN ARE DEAD AND GONE

97. SHE HASN'T THE KNACK

98. BALLYVOURNEY

99. JOHNNY MICKY'S

100. CAROLAN'S DRAUGHT

Ossian Publications produce a large range of Irish and Scottish Music for traditional & classical instruments as well as collections of tunes, songs, instruction books and items on the history of Irish Music.